# MEDITATION AND MINDFULNESS TRAINING

## PRACTICAL MINDFULNESS EXERCISES AND MINDFUL MEDITATIONS

By Best Selling Author
BETH BANNING

Published by Focused Attention, Inc.

Copyright © 2013

Mindfulness Icon from: radicalcourse.com

ISBN: 1492855235

ISBN-13: 978-1492855231

**Volume #3 of The Meditation for Life Series**

Other Books in this Series

**Volume #1: Meditation for Beginners:** Answers to Your Biggest Questions and Five Easy Meditations

**Volume #2: Meditation to Awaken Your Kundalini and Divine Life Force:** Including Chakra Meditation, Heart Meditation and Other Daily Meditations

# DISCLAIMER

All material in this book is intended for informational and educational purposes only. While every attempt has been made to provide information that is both accurate and effective, this book does not constitute medical or therapeutic advice for any medical or psychological condition.

In the presence of any medical or psychological history, or symptoms of any type, please seek the care of a physician. The author and publisher do not assume any responsibility or liability for damages of any kind resulting directly or indirectly from the implementation of information given in this book. Any use or application of the material in the following pages is at the reader's discretion and is the reader's sole responsibility.

# CONTENTS

# A FREE GIFT FOR YOU

Thank you for purchasing my book. I hope you find value in it. If so, please **Write Me a Review on Amazon**.

I greatly appreciate your feedback and your review will help others know if this book is right for them.

As a special *Thank You* for your interest in this book, I'd like to give you a free gift: *101+ Ways to Meditate*. Used in conjunction with *The Meditation for Life Series*, this supplementary resource will help you find the perfect ways for you to achieve a successful meditative state, tranquility, relaxation, peace of mind, and much more.

### Get Your Free Gift Right Now!

www.BethBanningAuthor.com/101-Meditations-Sign-Up

*"This material is priceless. It must've taken hours to find all these great meditations. The guided meditations are wonderful and if you're interested in meditation this is definitely a must-have resource."*
~ Dale Bach, author of *Mamma Trauma*

# INTRODUCTION

Mindfulness is a tool with which we can improve our lives and increase our awareness of living. With this tool we can gain many valuable insights into what life means and what living really is. So much of our lives are lost or pass by unnoticed because we allow ourselves to become distracted from the present, or insist on reliving moments that have passed and will never repeat themselves. We suffer and worry about what has not yet occurred and may never happen, and we make ourselves physically and mentally ill from the stress that is caused by losing control of the present moment and not using our minds in a positive way.

This book can be used by beginners and by people who are looking for new mindfulness techniques. For the beginner, I will introduce you to the concepts of mindfulness and explain how mindfulness can help you overcome numerous kinds of problems, including stress, relationship problems, and financial worries, just to name a few and will show how it can support you in many different aspects of your life. I will explain how mindfulness can be surprisingly simple, yet can bring lasting benefits. By reading this book you will discover how you can become more mindful using easy to memorize and practice techniques. You will also learn that by being mindful you can experience more peace, harmony, and happiness in your life and achieve higher levels of physical, mental, and spiritual well-being.

For the more advanced reader, this book can be an essential guide for finding new mindfulness techniques, all you need to do is flip to the section that says; Mindfulness Meditation: An Introductory Practice. From there on in the book you will discover many beneficial mindfulness practices for a variety of areas in your life.

Thank you for allowing me to support you on your mindfulness journey.

# THE WONDERS OF THE MIND

Our mind is an incredible thing. In ways, it is unknown and seemingly unknowable, and yet the human mind has driven us to achieve wonderful things, to build the civilization we see around us and create most of what we have and experience. The mind is an amazing thing yet, at the very same time, it can be a dangerous thing. It can be a great friend to us showing us the way, helping us through our day, conjuring up happy memories, giving us comfort through its ingenuity and capability for kindness and love. But also, the mind can be our own worst enemy, torturing and plaguing us with doubts and worst-case scenarios lifted out of nothingness.

We can be lifted with the powers of the imagination, or we can wallow and sink in nightmares, all a product of nothing more than the mind. The mind is one of our greatest tools, and to know how to use it to our advantage, and the advantage of those around us, can be a life-changing experience we are all capable of achieving.

We may think that we know the nature of our mind, but we cannot deny that the mind plays tricks on us. Stop for a moment and ask yourself if you truly 'know' your mind. Where is it located? What happens to it when we sleep or when we lose ourselves in abstractions of thought or intense physical activity? Can we trust our own mind, and if not, why not? Are we really aware of all the things that happen to us – such as the ideas and beliefs we take on unconsciously – or do most things pass to us and within us without notice or question?

## IS YOUR MIND WORKING FOR YOU OR AGAINST YOU?

What is undeniably sad about modern life is the fact that Western, so called 'developed' society, has so many ways of dulling the mind and preventing this magnificent organ from doing the job it was meant to do which is to help and support us in creating a peaceful, fulfilling, and loving existence. Our minds can be incredibly strong and can drive our will to overcome great obstacles and create great beauty. However, when our minds are not given the time to recover from all the overstimulation in which the majority of us spend most of our time, our minds become very fatigued and susceptible to fits of depression and states of anxiety, prone to worry and dwell on negative thoughts and feelings.

Unfortunately, this means that our overstressed minds often make us highly vulnerable, and this vulnerability leads to a wide range of problems that must be overcome in order for us to live happy, healthy, and fulfilling lives. This may sound a little far-fetched, but consider for a moment those things that trouble you or those thoughts that most often occupy your mind. Do you often worry? If so, what do you worry about? What does your mind do for most of the day? Are you using it to help improve your life, to create, and to explore? Or do you use it (as so many of us do) completing menial tasks in order to gain material reward so you can avoid worrying about the future, such as whether or not you can pay this month's bills?

# STRUGGLING IN THE MATERIAL WORLD

Simply switch on the television or spend some time browsing the Internet, and it will become abundantly clear how difficult it is in this modern age to maintain a healthy mindset. We are encouraged, if not driven, to live in a state of fear, distrust, and worry due to our society's pressures for perfection, comparison with others, and obsession with the "having more is better" mindset.

While this may seem fairly harmless, due perhaps to our familiarity with this situation, upon closer scrutiny it doesn't take long to realize the true implications of this state of affairs. Not only are we instructed – through advertising, movies, television – to believe that there are better and worse ways to look and act, we are also told that we should own certain things in order to prove our success and if we don't we are somehow incomplete, inadequate or unworthy.

Because of this struggle, many in our societies are plagued with mental disorders such as depression and anxiety. The numbers of people who live in almost constant stress has grown rapidly over the past few years, perhaps due in part to these unattainable aspirations we have been led to believe will make us happier and more fulfilled. Eating disorders and other such mental illnesses have become a frightening epidemic. This is another example of how our minds can be turned against us, but it need not be this way, because when we begin to become conscious and start to choose how we think and act, the world around us will almost immediately began to change for the better.

## THE MIND AND MINDFULNESS

It isn't difficult to understand why people are looking for solutions to stress, depression, and the emptiness millions of people experience due to the less than satisfying nature of modern life.

It is time for all of us wake up and begin to recognize the mind for what it is: a gift capable of producing beauty and understanding all that there is to understand. Why let another day pass without time spent gazing at the sunset and the beauty of the natural world in which we live, or another evening fall without stopping for a moment to tell yourself that you can achieve your potential?

Thankfully, this kind of awakening is spreading fast throughout the developed world as millions upon millions are realizing, and realizing quickly, that something needs to change in the way they view life and the world around them. People are beginning discover that, with the help of a few simple methods, they are perfectly capable of vast improvements in their day to day existence.

# A SOLUTION TO MANY PROBLEMS

So what is the solution to which so many people are turning? It comes in many forms, and it comes to us from ancient history and from distant lands. When we turn our mind to esoteric thoughts about the nature of our existence and our potential and begin to explore the knowledge of the soul and of the mind, there is one part of the world that we cannot help but notice. For thousands of years the people and cultures of India, Nepal, Tibet, parts of China, and other parts of the Far East have developed their knowledge and sciences of the soul, of self-awareness, and of our link with the divine. We in the West have an astonishing amount to learn from them.

While most people in Western civilization were living in little more than mud huts in the dark ages, the cultures of India were blossoming, producing some of the most beautiful and complex poetry mankind has ever seen. While those in Europe were engaged in endless feudal disputes and bloody territorial wars, the Indian and Tibetan sadhus and monks, holy men and sages were perfecting the art of meditation, achieving great feats of the mind, and overcoming the distractions of the world around them.

## THE ART OF MINDFULNESS

India, Tibet, Nepal... such countries have given birth to enlightened souls, hundreds and even thousands of years ago, people whose writings and teachings have developed and evolved alongside the ascent of mankind. But such countries do not have a monopoly on spirituality and meditative practices. You need not have been born there or grown up in that culture to benefit from the practices they produced, such as learning to exist completely in the present moment.

This – attending fully to the moment – is the essence of the art of mindfulness, a practice to which more and more people are turning to take control of their lives; lives which many people feel have spiraled downwards and become little more than a series of distractions, negative thoughts, and worries or dreads about the future. Mindfulness and mindfulness meditation is a solution to such ills of the soul; an ancient art perfected by the Tibetan Buddhists several centuries ago, and which still resonates with wonderful effect to this day. As with all forms of meditation, mindfulness is a free practice, one that can benefit absolutely everybody, from all walks of life and in all corners of the world.

Mindfulness means several different things, depending on who you ask. It is a practice, or set of practices, that have formed an important cornerstone of many of the meditative traditions that have arisen around the world. However, the term is mostly used to describe a particular set of practices used to achieve a specific goal – the sensation and benefits that arise when we remove all distractions from our minds, and focus on nothing but the very essence of a moment and our very being in time and space.

Indeed, it is the Western world, the more technologically developed countries with their stresses and fast pace of life, that require mindfulness and other such practices more than many others. It is a heartening reality that more and more people are beginning to wake up and explore the truth of their existence and to uncover the incredible things of which their bodies and minds are capable.

One of the truly wonderful things about the modern age is that the advent of freely available information and communication via the Internet has helped remind people that these other ways of being, these ancient and time-honored practices, are just waiting to be discovered and appreciated.

## OUR HABITUAL MINDLESSNESS

It is perhaps best to explain the notion of mindfulness by describing the opposite mode of being – that of 'mindlessness'. We have probably spent most of our lives in a mindless state. When we begin to think about our awareness of each day, and our actions and behaviors throughout our days, it becomes quickly apparent how mindless we can be. Think back to the last meal you ate, and just try to remember what happened in your mind during that time.

For the vast majority of us a meal begins with a plate of food, and before we know it, we look down to see an empty plate. The act of eating, enjoying, savoring or appreciating the meal itself has been lost, spinning away somewhere in a veritable sea of distractions and wandering thoughts. Driving too, or undertaking any journey, is another great and potent example of our day-to-day mindlessness. Quite often we arrive at our destinations without having any memory of what we were thinking most of that time or much awareness of the journey really having taken place, except for the sensation that time has passed, and we find ourselves in a different location.

Life these days is full of stressful decisions of carefully balancing different actions and different thoughts in our heads, like a plate-spinner dashing between poles, trying to keep everything moving at once so nothing tumbles down to the floor. Indeed, the majority of our time each day is spent worrying about things that have not yet happened, most probably will never happen or will not happen for a long time.

Our ability to exist within a present moment has been eroded, lost to habitual mindlessness. Just considering for a moment how much our mind is like a pinball machine with our thoughts bouncing between all the different things we have to worry or feel concerned about. Every once in a while we respond to our environment, which is like the flipper hitting the ball and sending it off in a new trajectory. From the pinball's perspective, this is a dizzying and depressing experience; bouncing between concerns about family, relationships, jobs, money, mortgages, and bills. Our mind ricochets like a ball between all of the things that distract us from living in the present moment. This prevents us from taking the time to consider who we really are, where and how we are, and what we are doing. The result of this mindlessness can be devastating.

By failing to live in, or be aware of the present moment, we miss so many positive experiences in our lives. We become fixated on thoughts of worst-case scenarios, on ghosts of the past and nightmares of the future. As mentioned before, it is the unquestioned ideas and beliefs we have taken on that cause us to fear so much - beliefs about being poor, being lonely, being inadequate – and these fears stop us from being mindful of our present situation, of how lucky we are or how beautiful our lives and surroundings may be in this present moment.

There is a reason for our mindlessness that is perhaps not just the fault our society and our unquestioned beliefs. Humans are, by their nature, inquisitive and have very active minds. We are easily distracted and always have been desirous of learning and creating new things. This is practically built into our very genes and points to a more instinctive way of being, and these natural tendencies probably wouldn't result in problems if we were living in a society and a civilization that nurtured our intrinsic nature or supported us to be at peace with ourselves and our circumstances. Unfortunately, this is not the case.

Given this, we must make a conscious choice to overcome our mindlessness. This choice is enacted by consciously choosing mindfulness and accomplished through mindful meditation and many other such practices. Mindfulness can only exist in the here and now. It is paying attention to where we are, who we are, what is happening, what we are feeling and thinking, and what we are doing. It is maintaining awareness of our lives and of our circumstances, and it is a balancing of our emotions and a calming of the turbulent nature of our minds. Mindfulness is clarity, it is inner peace, and as such it is the answer to many of the modern life's problems.

# MINDFULNESS OR MEDITATION, IT'S UP TO YOU

For thousands of years, meditation has proven itself to be a cornerstone of many civilizations. The ability to explore the inner space, to achieve a sense of tranquility and inner silence has brought inspiration, divine instruction, beautiful, and creative thoughts to individuals across the globe, many of whom went on to play important roles in history. However, meditation is much more than this, and meditative practices form a basic daily ritual for millions of people in the east. Indeed, a considerable percentage of the billion or so people who live in India undertake a period of meditation one or more times a day. In countries such as Nepal, Tibet, and elsewhere, meditation is as much a part of daily activity as is breakfast or getting dressed!

## THE DIFFERENCES

Meditation means many different things to many different people, but the most basic forms of meditation generally involve a combination of deep breathing exercises, bodily relaxation, and an effort made to turn one's thoughts inwards before attempting to remove all thoughts from the mind and then sinking into darkness, stillness, and silence. The idea is that by allowing ourselves to become as still and silent as possible, and by closing down the over-active mind, we can truly relax and soak ourselves in a quiet space where nothing can hurt us.

Where our problems and difficulties can melt away and begin to appear insignificant or even non-existent. There are dozens of different ways we can meditate, and meditation is something I highly recommend for everybody to explore and experiment with during their lives. Furthermore, meditation is now becoming increasingly recommended by medical professionals, doctors and practitioners due to the fact that there is increasing evidence suggesting that the health benefits of meditation are enormous, powerful, and long lasting.

Mindfulness, however, is not simply a form of meditation. While many of the same techniques as regular meditation can be used to achieve a mindful state of being, the reasons and objectives are essentially different. In most meditative practices, the reason for meditating is to more or less disappear within, to draw back from the world in which we live, and focus on the inner truths – the silence and stillness within. Most forms of meditation focus on disregarding the things that are around us. They help us pull away from the material world and remind ourselves that there is more to life than the material, tangible world. Mindfulness meditation is essentially the opposite of this.

It is about increasing our awareness of the 'here and now', of taking a moment to relax, yet to take stock, to awaken our senses to what it means to be alive. Mindfulness meditation is also about mindfully reminding ourselves of how fortunate we are to be alive or how fortunate we are to have certain things, certain abilities or gifts. It is aimed towards increasing confidence, increasing our capabilities and belief in our self by mindfully noticing and recognizing our achievements or how we develop. Mindfulness is a powerful tool that, when used wisely and correctly, can transform our lives by eradicating stress, worry, and negative anticipation. It can teach us to trust our senses and intuition and believe in our own capability to succeed.

# MINDFULLNESS VS. MINDFULNESS

The concept of mindfulness is one that, until a few decades ago, was mostly alien to the West. Our civilization has been built on concepts that are often at odds with mindfulness and the practice of living in the moment. Stopping and taking notice of where and who we are remains, for many people, somewhat odd or seemingly without purpose.

The Western world has always been preoccupied with the future goals and with the acquisition of status and material things. We put our inner thoughts and our feelings to one side and sacrifice our inner life – the realities of existence – in order to concentrate on getting on with our never-ending work, of acquiring more status and things, and of saving up for days to come. In short, mindfulness is something for which many have never found the reason or time, which is, in itself, a great pity.

Mindfulness has, over the past decade, become increasingly popular in the West and is currently being used by a wide range of people. It may have its origins in Tibet, but mindfulness is becoming an important tool in Western cultures to help see through the illusion and deal with the modern pace of life. Mindfulness practice has also been adapted by several important psychologists and therapists as a tool to help support people in the modern age.

# HOW WAS MINDFULNESS PRACTICE DEVELOPED?

Mindfulness and mindfulness meditation are the products of a very different culture, with a very different history. The eastern countries that have had the most influence over various esoteric practices such as mindfulness, have always placed a high level of importance on the workings of the mind. They have a belief system that is more compatible with the idea that by recognizing the existence of the mind as something that can be developed and nurtured, we can live happier and healthier lives.

Indeed, the cultures of India, Tibet, Nepal, and others that have been highly involved with the theories and writings surrounding the practice of mindfulness, have based their ideas about the nature of the mind on one extremely important idea – that of Maya. Maya is a Sanskrit word used to describe the world; the universe in which we live. It also means 'illusion', which is an important concept in all the major religions originating in these countries.

Ancient Hindu scholars wrote extensively of Maya, claiming that all we perceive around us is merely illusion, that we live in a world of shadows and dreams, and that we merely appear to be passing through this realm as we progress on our long journey back to oneness with the divine.

Tibetan Buddhists took this concept further asserting that one should attempt to be as disconnected as possible from the world we perceive to be real, and that suffering and difficulties in this life were a result of being too attached to the material aspects of existence. Today, millions of Hindus and Buddhists, as well as people of other religions, practice meditation as a way of momentarily escaping from Maya, from a material world of illusion and falsity, in order to reconnect with what is more fundamentally real.

# SEEING THROUGH THE ILLUSION

In many ways the practice of mindfulness arose from this type of meditation. This may seem somewhat contradictory. How can focusing on the present moment, focusing on existence and the purposeful nature of what we do, be connected to a belief that all that surrounds us is not real? Quite simply, it is because we spend so much time wrapped up in the illusion, carried along on a stream that is heading towards delusion and dissatisfaction, that taking the time to become aware of who we are, what we are, and what we are doing can help us focus on how to manage in this existence.

Mindfulness is about suspending self-criticism, removing judgment from our lives, and accepting circumstances for what they are. Mindfulness can even encourage us to laugh at Maya and find the whole cosmic illusion mildly ridiculous! If this sounds too flippant, consider that this way may be much preferable to finding yourself living in a constant state of worry!

# PASSIVE AND ACTIVE MINDFULNESS

As mentioned, meditation typically involves sitting still, breathing deeply, and concentrating. These three factors are used for the vast majority of meditative practices, and one can increase one's mindfulness by using this traditional form of meditation. Instead of removing all thoughts from one's mind while meditating, for mindfulness we focus solely on the action of breathing, of existing, and of living in the present moment. When it comes to cultivating a state of mindfulness, the traditional form of sitting in passive meditation is just one method we can use.

We can also cultivate mindfulness in all that we do, and every moment of the day's activities can be dedicated to this important state of being. For example, let us consider a woman who plays golf regularly and takes the sport fairly seriously. If she wished to cultivate mindfulness in herself while playing, she would be highly aware of each of her actions. She would take time to look at the green, to appreciate where she was and why she was there. She would be aware and mindful of the position of her body as she readied herself to take a swing, and she would be mindful of the fact that she needs to strike a physical balance between tension and looseness. Importantly, she would be aware that she absolutely has to live in the present moment, and not dwell on past failures, future successes or any unwanted memories that have a tendency to arise when we are trying to concentrate on the particular activity.

Perhaps the most important component of this golf analogy would involve what happens after the swing is taken. A person trying to cultivate mindfulness and a mindful way of being would accept that the previous moment has passed, that the consequences of the action (of the swing, in this example) cannot be changed, that the moment cannot be lived again. As a result of this mindset and with practice, no frustration, annoyance, anger or regret would arise, because the things that happened will never be different than they actually are – because they are now in the past and will never happen again. All attention would be on this next present moment.

The best part about cultivating mindfulness in your everyday life is that there is no right and no wrong about it. Even if you do get angry or frustrated, all there is for you to do is begin to notice that and then allow the energy of that frustration to move through you as you feel it. If your mind seems to get stuck in the energy of frustration, try shaking, jumping around or whatever is necessary to allow the energy of frustration to move through you and to cause your mind to get reconnected with the present moment.

The same analogy can be applied to almost any activity, and none of these techniques require you to meditate, be a master of any sort of yoga, although yoga is another superb and direct way to cultivate mindfulness, or any other esoteric eastern practice. The techniques required to cultivate mindfulness in everyday situations can be supported by:

# THE ABC'S OF MINDFULNESS:

## Allow.

The practice of mindfulness is the balancing act. As I have said, mindfulness is an art, not a science. Be sure not to try too hard, nor to try too little. Mindfulness does not come about by forcing yourself, nor by making no effort. Learning this balance is part of the practice. A heightened awareness of the details of your present reality is the first step. Do not resist anything that occurs, simply let things arise and respond with a sense of ease and flow. Let curiosity become your guide and allow yourself to enjoy the experience of simply being.

### Be Present.

Focus your attention on the details of your surroundings as well as paying close attention to your body and bodily sensations, and to the way it reacts to different stimuli. Notice what you experience when you are simply present. This is all about practicing and improving your ability to notice and feel what's going on in your mental state and physical form as well as in your environment. This is a practice of letting go of those distracting thoughts that are bound to come up and moment by moment bringing yourself back to this present moment.

### Concentrate.

Practice focusing your mind on what is happening now. Don't allow yourself to be distracted by either the past or the future. Keep bringing your mind gently back to an awareness of what is happening in this moment whenever you notice yourself drifting into distraction. Stay attuned to your present experience and allow what occurs naturally. Judging or wishing that things had occurred differently can cause much frustration, which is extremely counterproductive to the practice. Look for what gives you joy in this present moment and be very gentle with yourself. If you notice yourself judging or wanting things to be different, do your best to allow that desire to fall away. Know that what has happened was just perfect and happiness can only be found now, never in the past or in the future.

You can practice these ABC's of mindfulness during everything that you do – whether you are walking the dog, washing the car, eating a meal with friends or making your commute to work. By practicing these steps at different times of the day and in a multitude of situations, you can develop a healthy, mindful way of being that can greatly improve your life mentally, physically, and spiritually.

# THE BENEFITS ARE ENDLESS

Mindfulness practice can bring a wide range of benefits to anyone's life. Imagine being able to live comfortably, simply existing within the present moment, taking life as it comes, and to being free from regrets about the past, worries about the future or the constant barrage of self-criticism and second-guessing every situation!

Mindfulness teaches us to appreciate our place in the world, to step back from the incessant hubbub that surrounds us, and to learn to be grateful for our achievements. It allows us to be proud of what we do without constantly having to worry about what may or may not happen or whether we have done enough.

Additionally, developing a mindful way of being can help us stop or at least reduce our automatic habits that cause us pain. By being aware of what we are doing, we can take greater control over our actions, and thus our lives. In this way, mindfulness can be an effective solution to all manner of stress and any habitual reactions that you wish to improve.

## SITUATIONAL BENEFITS

Mindfulness can help us respond more desirably to all kinds of situations. It can help us learn to overcome problems in our relationships, with our finances, help us manage our anger, and even help with situations at work that may seem difficult to resolve. When we have the tools with which to see our world, and therefore the situations in our life, with more clarity, we are able to slow down and act more in harmony with our divine nature, instead of allowing things to prey on our minds and cause constant worry and stress. Mindfulness can also increase our level and capacity for creativity, and can help us achieve a more balanced and happy life.

On the other hand, when we allow our minds to be run by habitual ideas and beliefs we can easily get thrown out of balance. We can allow our "doing", our work or professional life, to overshadow all other things. Then simple pleasures, such as being outside in nature or among friends and loved ones, can become lost in our all too busy lives. Becoming mindful by creating a mindfulness practice also benefits us by making us more resilient. We are able to hear criticism in a whole new way, the pressures at work become less of a problem and we are able to more effectively concentrate on the tasks at hand, making us more efficient. With all this in mind, who wouldn't wish to cultivate their mindfulness?

## EVERYONE CAN PARTICIPATE

Everybody is capable of achieving a more mindful way of being, and as people in the world become more mindful, the world becomes a place of greater joy, presence, and peace. If more people participated in this practice, most of the pressures of the world would eventually begin to fade away, and in turn the competitive grinding nature of society would eventually begin to have less and less relevance for more and more people.

The beautiful thing about developing a higher level of mindfulness is that it requires nothing more than a little willpower, a little dedication, and a little daily practice. You don't need to buy any equipment and other paraphernalia in order to achieve what is actually a very human set of skills.

Simply carve out a few minutes one or more times each day to practice being aware of who you are, where you are, and what is happening. Begin by focusing on what you are doing, why you are doing it, and what it means to do it in that precise moment. As you cultivate this mindfulness practice you might notice changes right away, or it may take a little while, but either way mindfulness is guaranteed to bring enormous benefit to your life. Best of all no one is excluded from this practice – it's a gift any of us can give ourselves and enjoy.

# MINDFULNESS AND RELIGION

The original concepts of mindfulness came from the monasteries and ashrams of Tibet and northern India, where meditation was and remains an important aspect of living. For thousands of years the practices and techniques we now refer to as being part of mindfulness, have been undertaken by monks, sadhus, yogis, and others in the east, who consider the art of mindfulness a necessary skill for coping in the material world. For these and other people, life is simply a stage one has to get through on the long journey back to full spiritual awareness, back to being a part of god and one with all that is.

For many people, mindfulness certainly has a significant spiritual significance. Focusing on the present moment and meditating carefully on who we are and what we are doing is a powerful method for self-discovery, and a major step on the path to bliss and enlightenment, which is part and parcel of the spiritual realm.

For Buddhists particularly, mindfulness is required in order to live a life according to their faith, as it was one of the key techniques and modes of 'being' that was preached by Siddhartha Gautama (the Buddha himself) to his followers over two thousand years ago, after he achieved enlightenment. Buddhists believe that by practicing mindfulness in all that they do they can achieve balance within themselves and learn to cope with the suffering that is an inevitable part of living in this material world.

# YOU DON'T HAVE TO BE RELIGIOUS TO BENEFIT

However, for those of us who are not religious, are skeptical or even atheist, mindfulness is not something that should be avoided due to its origins in religious practice. Essentially, mindfulness is a deeply human practice, and one that need not have any religious affiliation to be practiced in the modern age. After all, why should the belief in some higher power, guiding hand or divine being have anything to do with the act of recognizing one's own existence and way of living in the moment? Indeed, most centers that teach mindfulness do so in a carefully secular manner, making sure to avoid any religious components that could cause confusion or put people off from participating.

In fact, nothing is really lost from mindfulness when religious or faith-based elements are taken out. Unlike some of the other eastern religious practices that have become popular in the West (forms of chanting, yoga, transcendental meditation, etc.), the practice of mindfulness and mindfulness meditation does not fundamentally change if used as part of a secular practice. Indeed, mindfulness has found much popularity and success in the Western world due in part to the fact that it can be used by people uninterested in eastern religious philosophy, without the burden or further study that some more religious practices demand.

Even the act of meditation requires no religious belief or faith. There is no reason why anyone cannot sit down, pull back from the hectic nature of the modern world, and quiet their mind. Mindfulness is particularly aimed at re-arranging the way we see our life and the world that surrounds us – it pays little attention to thoughts about the soul, spirit or afterlife. It is intended for the realization of inner understanding and it can be done anywhere at any time and need not entail anything mystical or elevated.

# IS MINDFULNESS DIFFICULT TO LEARN?

When we think about what mindfulness is and what it means, it seems as though it would be the easiest thing in the world to learn and master. After all, it is only the practice of heightening our awareness of particular moments in time, of being more conscious of our actions and our thoughts as they arrive and how they affect our experience of living. However, things aren't really that simple. The truth is that for most of us mindfulness, and developing a mindful existence, requires quite a lot of practice and may take some time to achieve full benefit.

There are those lucky people among us for whom mindfulness comes naturally. Occasionally, we hear of people who claim to have been able to achieve a mindful state of being from early childhood. Many of these special individuals have gone on to become teachers of mindfulness and have written extensively about their experiences and how it feels to be a natural at this art. It is to some of these people we owe our knowledge of mindfulness and many of the practices used today.

Unfortunately, the vast majority of us do not have this natural gift of mindfulness, and so we have to practice it in order to achieve the ultimate benefits that it offers us. However, that doesn't necessarily mean that mindfulness is difficult to learn. When we think of something as difficult, we usually understand it to take strenuous concentration or physical effort in order to achieve.

Mindfulness requires neither of these things. Rather, quite the opposite is true. Strenuous concentration is at odds with practicing mindfulness as this will undermine your ability to live and experience life joyfully in the present moment. Moreover, trying too hard to be mindful will defeat the object of mindfulness; it will create a sense of frustration within you, and frustration is the natural enemy, indeed, the very antithesis of all meditative and mindfulness practices.

When we become frustrated, we naturally create a mental blockage around the thing that is frustrating us. This means that when we return to try again, to re-attempt whatever we failed at previously, we will find it more difficult to achieve success as a result of the block caused by our own frustration.

This cycle is a difficult one to overcome; therefore, it is vitally important to be aware of this and be conscious about stopping before you become frustrated. This is why *focusing on acceptance* is so important. Should you feel frustration beginning to arise during any meditative process, or attempts at mindfulness, stop what you are doing, take a deep breath and sit silently for a moment. Remind yourself that frustration will not help you, that the moment in which you were frustrated has passed and will never arise or return again. This is hugely important, and something I would urge everyone interested in mindfulness to bear in mind at all times.

So mindfulness in itself is not difficult, and is not something that should take any concentrated effort. To be mindful, your mind needs to gently turn itself to the present moment. You need to lightly remove all distractions, while acknowledging both their existence and their relevance. You need to be relaxed, and to be aware at the same time.

While this isn't difficult, it requires time and patience. Keep your goal in mind, and remind yourself that this is something all of us can achieve. Continue to practice, and mindfulness will come eventually, you simply need to allow it to happen.

# HOW MUCH TIME DOES MINDFULNESS PRACTICE TAKE?

There is, of course, no set amount of time that it takes to practice mindfulness. As mentioned, some individuals are able to turn their minds to mindfulness easily and without effort, while for other people; it may take months or years before they are able to say that they are living continuously in a mindful state.

One of the key things about mindfulness is that you shouldn't spend any time anticipating what may or may not happen in the future. Wondering when or if mindfulness will reveal itself in your life is fundamentally opposed to the concept itself. We simply must be is gentle, patient, and accepting – each moment comes and goes, and leaves its trace – our goal is to be fully present to these moments before letting them go to become part of the past.

By spending a little time each day either meditating mindfully, or being actively mindful in the things that you do, we should be able to notice subtle differences in our mindset that, before long, become large and significant changes that effect the way we live and see the world around us. Simply taking fifteen to twenty minutes each day to be purposefully mindful can make a significant difference – before long, we'll discover that we are seeing things with more clarity, and letting go of regrets and worries about what may have happened differently in the past.

It shouldn't be long before your mindfulness practices start to bear this fruit.

The main difference noticed by people who practice mindfulness is that they cease to worry about the future, accepting things as they happen for what they are. To worry about the future is to worry about a phantom, a shadow or an illusion. Until it occurs, the future is little more than a figment of our imagination, something we can only speculate about.

A little mindfulness each day will enormously help to put such things into perspective, and it won't be long before the benefits of this new perspective begin to show themselves. This seems like quite an incredible feat for the majority of us. Yet, even a few minutes of simple mindfulness practice each day can help to erase these worries as you learn to bring focused attention to the perfection of the moment.

Ready to get started?

# A SIMPLE WALKING MINDFULNESS MEDITATION

Let's start with something most of us do every day. From the moment you wake up to the time you go to bed you walk from one place to another. Walking can be a wonderful reminder to become mindful.

To start your mindfulness meditation, begin by planning your route. This could be as simple as walking up and down the stairs in your house or around your living room. If you choose to go outside, in the initial phases of practicing mindfulness it's best to map out a route that is a level, open, and as disturbance-free as possible.

Once the route is set, start in a normal standing position with arms hanging comfortably at your sides, crossed or clasped in front of you or behind you, whatever feels most normal and natural to you. If you're going outside, and weather and terrain permitting, barefoot is a wonderful way to do a walking mindfulness meditation because you also get the added benefits of what is called 'Earthing,' but that's a subject for another whole book.

Your eyes should remain softly open with a study unfocused gaze looking down at the ground a few feet in front of you. This will help you stay internally focused.

Start walking, and as you do remain aware of the ABCs of mindfulness:

## Allow.

The practice of mindfulness is the balancing act using not too much effort nor too little. Maintain a heightened awareness of the details of your present reality. Do not resist anything that occurs, simply let things arise and respond with a sense of ease and flow. Let curiosity become your guide and allow yourself to enjoy the experience of simply being.

## Be Present.

Focus your attention on the details of your surroundings as well as paying close attention to your body and bodily sensations, and to the way it reacts to different stimuli. Practice improving your ability to notice and feel what's going on in your mental state and physical form as well as in your environment. Let go of distracting thoughts that come up and bring yourself back to this present moment.

## Concentrate.

Practice focusing your mind on what is happening now. Keep bringing your mind gently back to an awareness of what is happening in this moment whenever you notice yourself drifting into distraction. Look for what gives you joy and when you notice yourself judging or wanting things to be different, do your best to allow that desire to fall away. Remember that happiness can only be found in the now.

As you do your walking meditation you can alternate between simply noticing the general sensations of how you feel without involvement and then letting these go, and then zooming your focus in on a very specifically sensation, like your feet touching the ground. This rotating of your focus keeps the practice fresh and helps you to avoid mental distractions and to stay more present in the moment.

# CREATING YOUR UNIQUE PRACTICE

As you're developing your own unique practice, remember that with any form of meditation or esoteric practice, regular undertaking is of utmost importance. Most of us have spent our entire lives being run by unquestioned ideas and beliefs. For years and years, we have lived our lives by mostly unconscious rules and conditioning. It can take months or even years, to change this mental behavior and adapt our ways of thinking to become more positive, peaceful, and ultimately more mindful.

We are extremely accustomed to shutting out both the outside and inside world, to ignore our feelings as they rise and fall, and to suppress our negative emotions until they erupt in unhealthy outbursts of depression, anger, and self-criticism. This is why practicing mindfulness as often as possible is very important.

## TURNING THE ORDINARY INTO THE EXTRAORDINARY

I've said that practicing mindfulness isn't necessarily a difficult thing to do; although it may take some time before the act itself becomes natural and automatic. We can do anything mindfully if we choose to: when we wake up in the morning we can make a mental note to examine and think carefully about the way we feel, to explore the sensation of waking up, reflect on the dreams that are dwindling in our sleepy minds. We can dress ourselves mindfully, examining the sensations of putting on fresh clothes or the feelings the different colors and textures evoke in our minds.

Eating breakfast, traveling to work, working on specific tasks, and returning home can all be done in a mindful fashion, all of which can become much more worthwhile because of the practice. Mindfulness isn't only something achieved through specific exercises – it can be something we embrace actively as a part of our lives; something we attempt to do all of the time.

It is important to practice a little bit every day, to turn mindfulness into something of a daily routine. With this in mind, look at your daily routine and identify at least three things that you do every day without exception. Pick at least one of these activities and commit to turning it into one of your daily mindfulness practices.

Each day is different. Each sunrise will only ever happen once before fading away and never, ever happening again. One of the most important factors of mindfulness is that each moment is unique – even brushing your teeth – and will only occur one time in our lives. When you take routine daily activities and turn them into mindful experiences of the moment, you allow yourself to relax, be present, and see, feel, and hear things that might surprise you. There is extraordinary beauty and elegance in every moment, but only if we are open to it.

## HOW LONG AND HOW OFTEN?

Of course your practice will move along more quickly if you commit to a regular routine, spending a minimum of ten to fifteen minutes a day focused on mindfulness. If you don't have time to consistently practice, and indeed, for many of us this is very difficult, don't become disheartened. For a lot of us, we simply need to spend certain parts of the day concentrating on other things, be it work or something in our home life. However, we can integrate mindfulness techniques and practices into these activities, simply by stopping for a moment in the middle of a task, taking a deep and purposeful breath, and reminding ourselves "this is me, this is where I am, and this is what is happening." This needn't take more than a second or two, but when you remember to be conscious and bring your attention to the fact that everything you do only ever happens in the present moment it can make a significant difference.

Simple breathing exercises are also an excellent way of practicing the ABCs of mindfulness at regular intervals throughout the day, as breathing is something we do all of the time, but are mostly unaware of as we do it. When you find yourself being tense or uncomfortable in any way, use this as a reminder to take a deep, slow, purposeful inward breath. Try to hold the breath for a second or two longer than you normally would. Feel your lungs fully inflated inside your chest before releasing slowly, purposefully, and easily. Again, feel your lungs for a second or two as they are fully deflated, and repeat. This time, when your lungs are full, take a moment to realize that you are breathing, that you are breathing the air that surrounds you.

You can also take a bit of time to focus on the sensation of your breath moving through your body. Be aware that the breath you have inhaled is traveling outwards from your chest through your body replenishing, energizing, and bringing much needed oxygen to all of your cells and various body parts. This is a simple, easy exercise that you can do throughout the day, no matter what you are doing, and one that in only a few minutes a day can increase your level of mindfulness.

## DON'T WAIT; START NOW!

There are many different ways to begin a successful mindfulness practice, and you are undertaking one of them at this very moment by reading about it. There is plenty of literature available these days that gives ideas and passes on wisdom surrounding mindfulness, and these writings are an excellent place to start. A little research will reveal that there are various religious, scientific, and psychological approaches to mindfulness, each designed to suit different people with various needs and requirements. It is a wise thing to explore each of them and discover how one or more of these many forms of mindfulness may help you accomplish what you want to achieve.

To begin a committed mindfulness practice requires a bit of thought and a bit of soul searching. One of the methods recommended for mindfulness beginners is to think carefully about the many moments of our day in which we are mindless so we can begin to realize just how much time passes without us really noticing it. How many times throughout the day are we essentially on auto-pilot, lost in our thoughts, and meandering our way through life without even looking up at our surroundings?

Many of us will find this list represents most of our waking day as so much of our time is spent in a mindless state where we are little more than sleepwalkers, exactly what we hope to change by being more aware of each passing moment. This exercise may also help to compile another list, one in which we write down those things we would like to worry less about.

This sort of list usually involves concerns about finances, our relationships, our families or our social or sexual lives. It can be enormously helpful to take a good look at a list like this, as it should become quickly apparent how much better your life would be if you were free from worry about many of the things on such a list. It's helpful to notice that we are alive even as we write such lists. We, breath, exist and experience the freedom and ability to write, to think, and to consider. This is what mindfulness asks us to focus on, the moment in which we live.

## PREPARING FOR MINDFULNESS MEDITATION

When it comes to mindfulness, there are certain things we can do to prepare ourselves. Mindfulness meditations are one of the most immediate and direct practices we can undertake to cultivate our mindfulness. As such, I highly recommend that you partake in meditative practices of this sort. As with all types of meditation, mindfulness meditation requires a certain amount of time and space set aside for the practice, as it is generally not something that we think to do in the spur of the moment.

Meditation is most successful when we have a designated space in which to meditate. This needn't be anything fancy, and it can simply be a corner of a room or a part of a garden. It should, however, be somewhere that we feel comfortable and safe, and somewhere that we are unlikely to be disturbed or distracted.

Meditation spaces should be, as far as is possible, somewhere reserved primarily for meditation. This is due to many factors, and some people believe that the act of meditating has a positive effect on a physical space itself, on the energies that accumulate there. Whether you believe this or not, it is well understood that by having a designated meditation spot, you can slip into a meditative state more easily each time you return there.

This space should be quiet, tranquil, comfortable, and free as possible from physical and subtle disturbances. Many people find that the almost inaudible hum of electrical appliances and even radio signals can disturb their meditations, and as such, if possible all machinery and electrical item should be switched off in your meditation space.

# MINDFULNESS MEDITATION: AN INTRODUCTORY PRACTICE

Mindfulness meditation is, as mentioned, the most direct way to nurture a sense of mindfulness, which can enhance our enjoyment and appreciation of this life and this world in which we live. There are many, many ways to meditate mindfully, and it is well worth your time to explore several of these methods and to experiment with mixing and matching different techniques until you find one that suits your needs, temperament, and abilities. However, no matter how familiar you are with meditation, it is always helpful to begin with a basic technique you can build on over time.

The first stage of this, and almost all meditative practices, is to relax the body and the mind. One of the most effective ways of doing this is by sitting down in an upright position, and allowing your body to become comfortable and calm. By sitting cross-legged we can relax many of our key muscles and align the energies of the body. Do not allow yourself to be rigid or tense, but try not to become too relaxed or loose, either. Breathe deeply a couple of times, and check that you are comfortable.

Begin by taking some deep inward and outward breaths. Follow the path of your breath as it spreads outwards from your fully inflated lungs, out into your shoulders and tummy, and then exhale all of the breath out from your body, until your lungs are completely deflated. Hold the breath for a couple of seconds longer than you normally would, and then breathe in again. Continue to follow the breath outwards, and focus your attention on the oxygen, the life force moving up and down your body, out to your arms and legs, your hands and feet, until your entire form is energized and filled with this vital life force.

Concentrate on the action of breathing. Focus for a moment on how odd it is that we can be constantly doing something so important, and yet so unconscious of it! This is precisely the kind of thing we are trying to overcome through mindful meditation. Continue to breathe deeply and focus on the breath until you feel increasingly more relaxed and stable, comfortable and calm.

With most forms of meditation, the next step would be to begin allowing all thoughts to fall away, and to bask in silence and stillness, attempting to achieve complete emptiness of mind. Not so with mindfulness meditation, as to do so would not be a mindful exercise. Instead, we continue to focus on what we are doing, and where we are. We are breathing; we are sitting in a room. We are in a physical place, we are alive, and we are practicing our mindfulness.

Unlike these forms of meditation that ask us to let all thoughts to fall away, which therefore are facilitated by keeping our eyes closed, a mindfulness meditation can actually be enhanced by allowing your eyes to remain open and by keeping a soft steady gaze directly in front of you.

Feel your bottom sitting on the floor, cushion or chair, your feet under your legs, and the air rushing in and out of your nostrils. Perhaps there's a slight breeze on your skin – notice it. How does it feel? Try not to look around the room if possible, simply be aware that it is there, and you are within it. Outside the room is a whole world, a whole universe, and each second is passing by as time continues on, moment by moment. And you are there, in your room, being aware that each moment is coming, being experienced by you, and passing away.

Our minds are busy things, turbulent and rarely calm. Trying to empty the mind of distracting thoughts is an incredibly difficult thing to do. No matter how much we try to focus on nothing but that which is happening in this moment, most of us find that we are constantly interrupted by memories, emotions rising and falling, snippets of songs, jokes, scenes from films, ideas for things we may or may not have said, and thoughts about the future.

When we are meditating mindfully, we must at first accept that this is the case – that thinking is something that happens and that will most likely happen during your meditation. Should these sorts of thoughts enter your head simply notice them when they happen. Acknowledge them. Tell yourself quietly and gently, 'that was a thought' or 'thinking is occurring,' and reassure yourself that this is natural, almost inevitable. Do not dwell on the thoughts as they come and go. Do not allow yourself to get lost in what has been or may be.

Merely acknowledge the arrival of each thought and do not worry about it when it leaves. If you notice you have become caught up in your thoughts, make an effort to pull your mind back to the present, back to the room, and back to your breathing.

This sort of exercise should be practiced for fifteen minutes or so every day. After it becomes more and more comfortable and natural feeling, you can extend this length of time comfortably and gradually, until you are meditating this way for half an hour, forty five minutes or even an hour.

The aim of this exercise is to increase your capacity for mindfulness and to practice being yourself just as you are experiencing the world just as it is. As soon as you start grasping for an idea of what this form of meditation is supposed to be, or what it may be to someone else, and projecting this onto yourself, it won't yield the positive results you want and you may find yourself falling into a pattern of frustration. Do your best not to become frustrated or worried about your progress, and if you do, just notice the frustration or concern as it occurs. Don't attempt to push the frustration or worry away or to empty your mind completely, just notice the thoughts as they come and go.

# STRESS AND MINDFULNESS

Stress is one of the great plagues of the modern age. Left unchecked, stress can cause not only significant mental difficulties but can also manifest itself in a range of physical ailments, such as: heart disease, ulcers of the stomach, and problems of the kidneys, liver, and respiratory and circulation systems. A huge number of other common, yet dangerous ailments can also result from stress.

Mindfulness is one of the most effective cures for stress as it equips us with the tools to view life and existence just as it is. By being mindful, we can effectively 'step back' from our problems and the sources of our stress, and see them in a new light and from a new perspective. This change of perspective can help us see new possibilities that we would never have noticed before.

Stress can be enormously reduced by practicing simple, daily, mindfulness meditations. Whenever you feel stressed, be sure to take some time out each day to unwind, to enjoy some peace and quiet, and for a few moments of contemplation. Take a minimum of fifteen minutes after work or in the morning, to sit in your meditation spot, and focus on the act of breathing, on the presence of being, and on the moment as it happens.

## A MINDFULNESS PRACTICE TO HELP ALLEVIATE STRESS

Whether you know it or not you have the ability to leave your stresses at the door, to leave your worries outside your home. You can practice this by consciously and literally telling yourself to do so, and then spending a few minutes being present and mindful of your surroundings.

Before you walk through the front door of your home or the door to your room, say to yourself in a quiet voice, "From this moment on, I will exist only in the present moment. I am leaving my worries and problems outside this sacred space". Take a deep breath, and as you step over your threshold, exhale fully and purposefully. Then, mindfully enter your house, and begin looking around consciously noticing all the details of the room. Feel your feet on the floor, your shoes on your feet, and your clothing touching your body. Notice the air moving in and out of your nostrils and be thankful and aware of where you are, and of the safety and comfort of your home.

Allow yourself a minimum of five minutes each day to cultivate this sense of mindfulness and your ability to leave your worries behind – if even for these few moments. Allow yourself the time to feel the sense of gratitude you have for your existence and for your ability to be present.

# MINDFULNESS AT WORK

For many of us, our jobs or work-places are difficult settings to be in. Because there are so many things to 'do,' they are often the places where we slip into patterns of mindlessness, without realizing it. Mindlessness in the workplace can lead to a wide range of problems, as this way of being quickly leads us to lose a feeling of satisfaction or a sense of pride or purpose in our work. With this mindset we can easily begin to see ourselves as unlucky and begin to feel bored, unsatisfied or little more than an automaton, completing tasks of little interest to us.

Companies do not perform well with workers who are mindless, and there has been much corporate interest in using and promoting mindfulness as a practice with which to boost well-being, productivity, efficiency, and effectiveness in the workplace. But how can you practice mindfulness while working? Many people claim that there aren't enough hours in the day already and so they will never find time to add a mindfulness practice. However, with a bit of careful consideration, it soon becomes clear that your typical working day is full of moments that are ideal for mindfulness meditations and practices.

## A MINDFULNESS PRACTICE TO HELP YOU AT WORK

As you sit in your car on your way to work or when you are waiting for commuter transportation, use these times as moments of mindfulness and concentrate on your breathing, paying attention to where you are physically and the activities around you. Can you feel a soft seat beneath you? Are you outside, in the open air? What is happening around you? How do you feel? Quietly and mindfully make a mental note of who and where you are, not thinking of what is ahead of you in the day or the difficulties the day may bring, but just place your attention on the moment you are living in and nothing else.

At regular intervals throughout the workday, find opportunities to pay close attention to your various bodily sensations, the feelings running through your form, and any aches or pains you may be experiencing. This might be when you're walking from one place to another or when you're waiting for some task to complete itself. Concentrate on releasing tension from your body, take a minute out from what you are doing, and focus on each part of your body in turn. Breathe deeply, and feel each and every part of your body relaxing, relieving itself of any tension you may not have even noticed.

Try eating your lunch alone and in absolute silence. Instead of distracting yourself by reading, watching, or talking with others while you eat, savor each mouthful and concentrate on the experience of eating. Feel the textures and enjoy the flavors on your tongue; recognize the way your body reacts. Eating mindfully is an excellent way to nurture a mode of mindfulness in our lives and this can easily be done at work.

Use your breaks as a real break. At least twice a week, spend a little time outside on your break if possible, in a park or any available green space. Sit down; look at the world around you while you focus on existing – on the moment of being.

You may want to find some mindfulness buddies at work, people with whom you can share your meals or break times in a mindful manner. Having a small community of like-minded people can help support you in remembering to focus your attention on being mindful throughout the day. Even just seeing one of your mindfulness buddies can bring your attention back to your practice of mindfulness, even if only for a few moments.

As with all areas of your life, the opportunities for practicing mindfulness in your work setting are only limited by your imagination and your desire to experience the benefit of mindfulness in your life.

# MINDFULNESS AND YOUR GOALS

We all have ambitions, those goals we would love to achieve in this lifetime. For many of us, certain things seem to keep getting in the way; stopping us from stepping closer to realizing our dreams. In these sorts of situations mindfulness can be of great help, and having a more mindful mode of being is one way of ensuring you are moving closer in life towards those ambitions you wish to fulfill.

Often, we find ourselves mindlessly repeating bad habits or destructive, negative behaviors. We sometimes don't even realize we are doing something that is not serving us or responding habitually to something, until it is much too late.

How many times have you turned down an opportunity because you were unreasonably fearful of what the consequences of accepting may have been? How many times have you been too distracted to be polite or courteous to somebody, who could potentially help you in the future? How many times have you approached a situation with a negative or pessimistic attitude, often without any reason other than that a similar situation had left a bad taste in your mouth previously? All such actions and reactions are examples of mindlessness, and as such they can hinder our progress towards achieving our goals.

By practicing mindfulness daily we can encourage our brain to become increasingly mindful, until this becomes our default setting. When we approach situations mindfully, we are fully aware of what is happening, what is being said, and how we are responding.

We find ourselves thinking with more clarity, responding in a more balanced and positive way, and generally having more self-confidence. This is due in part to the fact we are not allowing ourselves to be dragged down by bad memories of previous experiences and worries about the future. By instilling mindful responses and actions into our lives, we eliminate negative habits and stop allowing ourselves to act in an automatic, thoughtless, or distracted manner.

Practicing mindfulness in the moment will allow our attention to focus on just what is happening, how we are in relation to that, and what we want, as I am fond of saying, what you focus your attention on will grow. In essence, regular mindfulness, and simple mindfulness practices such as meditation or silent contemplation will bring your thinking, your actions, and therefore your life into alignment with your goals.

## A MINDFULNESS PRACTICE TO HELP ACHIEVE YOUR GOALS

Developing a mindful awareness of any kind of emotional discomfort is an excellent tool you can use to support your goals. We are energetic beings and energy wants to move. Our unquestioned beliefs, opinions, and judgments block energy and cause us discomfort. Mindfulness is an excellent way to support the unblocking of stagnant energy and opening yourself to new possibilities for achieving your goals.

The next time you notice yourself feeling uncomfortable in any way, STOP before you speak or act. Find a quiet place where you can become present to your emotional discomfort – the blocked energy. It's best to do this exercise when the emotional discomfort is happening, but if you can't do it in the moment, as soon possible write down what happened and how you're feeling and do this exercise later when you have time.

While either sitting or standing, become present to this discomfort as though it were an ' object of art' in your physical body. Notice where the discomfort is located in your body, and then identify its characteristics. Ask yourself, if it had a shape, what would it be? If this discomfort had a color, a temperature or a texture what would they be?

Once you become very present to your discomfort, close your eyes, if they weren't already, and begin to feel this object moving down from where it was originally located. Feel or imagine it slowly moving, down, down, down – down through your legs, out the souls of your feet, and into the ground below you. Then imagine this object moving deep, down into the ground and dissolving into the earth.

If you have a hard time visualizing or imagining this, just pretend that you can.

Once you've seen this object dissolve completely, open your eyes and become present to this moment, free from emotional discomfort. Now, from this sense of spaciousness and freedom from upset, choose what you are going to do or say in relation to the situation that stimulated your discomfort.

Being able to act from this quality of clarity and connection to the present moment will support you in making decisions and taking actions that are in harmony with what is truly most important to you. Taking actions with this quality of mindfulness will help ensure that whatever you do and say will be most likely to support you in achieving what you want to accomplish.

# MINDFULNESS AND DEPRESSION

Depression is quite a difficult thing to define; it is used as an umbrella term for a wide range of mental disorders, which range from mild and fairly manageable, to devastating and life debilitating. Depression has truly become an epidemic in many modern cultures.

According to the Mayo Clinic, no one knows the exact causes of depression. As with many mental disorders, it seems a variety of factors may be involved. One of the factors they have discovered is that certain events; such as, high stress situations, the death or loss of a loved one, and financial problems – just to name a few – can trigger depression in some people. This type of depression can be significantly improved with mindfulness.

I am not suggesting that you use mindfulness in lieu of your doctor's advice. What I am suggesting is that mindfulness, when used in conjunction with any traditional medical advice, can be very beneficial.

To understand why mindfulness can help with depression, we must examine why depression sometimes arises, and then spirals out of control. Some forms of depression result from excessive worries about the future and regrets about the past. These worries and regrets are often turned inward resulting in guilt and shame about what might've happened if we had only done something different or not being good enough to handle what might happen in our current situations.

When we become depressed it's as if we have tunnel vision – our world becomes reduced to a narrow, negative, depressing reality. We may not even notice when the depressive cycle begins, and we only come to recognize it when it is too late. Mindfulness meditation and general mindfulness practice can significantly help us realize when depression is beginning to set in, and help us nip the problem in the bud. Furthermore, having a greater awareness of our thoughts and of the world around us can significantly help us put any problems into perspective by helping us to see the bigger picture.

Mindfulness gives us the ability to live in the present and to see reality more clearly, eradicating the ghosts of the past or specters of days yet to come. Also, it teaches us not to shun and suppress negative thoughts and emotions when they arise, but to be present to them and see them as just small parts of our moment-to-moment existence. It helps us see emotions as experiences that come and then go just as quickly when we let them. This way, emotions don't take us by surprise, causing us to resist them, and instead we learn to embrace them as just another powerful indication that we are alive.

But how do we achieve this state of being and stop ourselves from sinking into depression or being caught up in negativity? As I have said before, we do not necessarily have to stop our thoughts or empty our minds as we might do in more conventional meditative practices. Indeed, quite the contrary is true – if you want to find a way of being mindful in order to overcome depression, you need to train your mind to be almost hyper-aware of what is happening in it in each present moment. When your attention is focused solely in the present moment, it is impossible to have fears about the future or regrets about the past.

Mindfulness is entirely about the moment, the present, the immediate. In each moment that comes, one after another, there is no past and there is no future. It is almost bizarre when we realize it, but we can only live in the present; the past is unreachable, unchangeable, and the future is unknowable. All we can experience is what is happening right here, and right now. Realizing this is a highly effective way of dealing with any sort of negative thoughts, regrets or worries, and can produce a level of tranquility and happiness in our lives that will cause us to wonder how we ever survived without it.

## A MINDFULNESS PRACTICE TO HELP OVERCOME DEPRESSION

Very often situational depression is caused by self-judgment and dissatisfaction with ourselves. For this reason it is very helpful to focus your mindfulness practice on yourself in a nurturing and loving way. Mindful self-massage is a wonderful way to help you not only become very present in the moment, but also to become more familiar with the extraordinary being that you are.

Begin this exercise by setting aside no less than fifteen minutes and finding a quiet place that you feel comfortable and will not be disturbed. Your meditation area may be ideal.

1. Start by taking three or four slow deep breaths to relax yourself. As you do, feel the air coming into your lungs as they fill up to capacity. As slowly and consistently as possible, on each exhale, push all the air out of your lungs.

2. Take a moment and scan your body, and identify an area that you can reach easily and that is tense or sore and in need of attention.

3. Tighten and release the muscles in that area. As you do, feel each contraction in that area. Pay attention to how your muscles respond to the contraction. As you release feel not only the muscle, but the energy now flowing in

the muscle. Continue this for at least 30 seconds paying very close attention to each sensation that you feel.

4. Now, use your thumb, knuckles, or fingertips to massage the muscles in this area. In a strong yet gentle way; start to massage the muscle with whatever pressure is comfortable for you. Move the pressure around in small circles all the way around the muscle. Pay close attention to the sensations you're feeling as you massage yourself. What is the pressure like? How does your skin feel underneath your touch? What is the temperature of your skin – is it warm, cool?

5. Now use your whole hand to massage this area. Squeeze the muscles, hold and then release. Be aware of how your body feels with every movement of your hand.

6. Pay attention to how your touch affects your whole body. Do you feel more relaxed? Is your body looser? Has the temperature of your body changed?

7. When this area feels more relaxed, nurtured, and loved, it's time to move to another part of your body. Scan your body again for tension or soreness.

8. Move on to the next area. Continue this process for a minimum of 15 minutes or until you feel relaxed and present.

When you've completed focusing your mindfulness practice on yourself in this gentle and nurturing way, take time to feel the sense of loving kindness this has created in your awareness. Rest in this space of comfort and enjoyment, recognizing that in this moment there is nothing wrong and you can feel satisfied. Take some time to anchor this sensation into your being so that you can recall it at other times when your mind begins to distract you with thoughts of self-judgment or fear about the future. Creating strong anchors in your awareness such as this can help keep you from being dragged away by the currents of depression.

# MINDFULNESS AND RELATIONSHIPS

It seems all too true that matters of the heart are extremely prone to mindlessness. If you are in a long term relationship with someone, it becomes extremely easy to begin to take them for granted and to stop appreciating them or having sensitivity towards their feelings, their needs or their emotional well-being.

Conversely, if we are swept up with the mad impulses and impetuous longings of a new relationship, we can become so distracted that we fail to see the many warning signs reality is offering us that, if we were mindful, would steer us clear of developing a relationship doomed to fail.

Mindlessness in a relationship is a sure path towards failure and heartbreak. However, by being more mindful with a partner, we can improve all aspects of a relationship, from making it more tender and loving, to improving sexual relations, to making it more trusting and honest, and even to achieving shared goals and ambitions.

## A MINDFULNESS PRACTICE TO HELP WITH YOUR RELATIONSHIP

All too often many relationship problems occur because we speak too much, too quickly. I suggest you review the mindfulness practice relating to emotional discomfort that I covered in the previous section on goals. You'll see that making this a regular practice in your relationship can have great benefit. Emotional discomfort turns into a problem whenever we are not mindful enough to get present and centered in the present moment. Begin to practice mindfulness in your relationships by slowing down physically and mentally, especially when there is any sense of emotional discomfort.

To be mindful physically, begin by recognizing and feeling the sensations in your body. If you become angry or frustrated, your body responds in physical ways. Your muscles tighten, your jaw clenches, your breathing quickens, and your pulse races. Stop for a moment, breathe, and recognize that these changes are taking place inside you without you consciously having allowed them to happen. Mindfully becoming present to these changes will allow you to control them, and will help you settle down.

It can take up to twenty minutes for the chemicals released from an intense feeling of anger or frustration to fully dissipate from your body. Even longer if you keep pouring the fuel of rampaging thoughts on this fire.

To be mindful mentally, begin to use your speech as your mindfulness practice. There is a national campaign called T.H.I.N.K., which forms an acronym that works wonderfully as a mindfulness exercise. The T.H.I.N.K. campaign challenges you to ask yourself: Is my communication (what I am saying, texting or typing):

**True**

**Helpful**

**Important**

**Necessary**

### Kind?

I strongly suggest that you memorize this acronym, and then in moments of emotional distress you practice the mindfulness of considering how your last or next communication measures up to each letter in the acronym.

If it doesn't, then stop and rethink what you just said or what you were about to say. How could you say or restate this in a way that reflects the T.H.I.N.K. characteristics, but still gets your point across? This simple mindfulness practice can quickly and easily help create better relationships in every area of your life.

# MINDFULNESS AND ANGER

We all experience anger at some point in our lives, but for many of us it is an all too common and seemingly unavoidable pitfall of existence, something that crops up much more than we like. Nobody enjoys being angry. Being angry repeatedly can cause high levels of stress and puts a huge amount of strain on our bodies and minds. Indeed, anger problems are quickly and quite drastically followed by real and often devastating health problems. Being unable to control our anger is an important issue for many people. For this reason, millions of people have sought help with their ability to manage anger.

Unfortunately, anger doesn't exist in a vacuum – it is a response to an environmental stimulus. Many of us are fortunate enough to live or work in relatively stress-free situations, but there are those of us who are not so lucky, and who slip into cycles of frustration and anger that are difficult to get out of. Difficult, because in the heat of the moment, being angry feels like a release from the situation, a solution to the negative stimulus. Of course, the anger itself is never a solution and merely serves to worsen any given problem.

Thankfully, mindfulness is a great way to help with anger management, because it gives us the tools with which to step back from our immediate, hyper-emotional, and mindless reactions. When we are mindful we consider our situation, what we are doing, and how we are feeling. We recognize the physiological changes that take place in our bodies as we become angry, and thus we can calm them. We have a heightened sense of self-awareness when we are mindful, and as such, we can remain conscious and T.H.I.N.K. about how we want to respond. Through this self-awareness, our level of clarity increases, our choices and actions become more harmonious, and as we gain a healthier, more mindful perspective, our emotions respond accordingly.

## A MINDFULNESS EXERCISE TO HELP MANAGE ANGER

One excellent method for heightening self-awareness and mindfulness about our response to stimulus in our environment is by listening to music. Most often we listen to music quite mindlessly, as a distraction or as something in the background. As we listen to music, mindfully, we should concentrate on each vibration, and recognize the emotions it stimulates and as each note passes through us.

For this exercise, select three or four different pieces of music – ones that evoke very different emotional feelings. As an example some songs evoke a more emotional response while others stimulate you mentally, some are more relaxing or energetic, boring or invigorating, soothing or irritating. Pick pieces of music that really run the gamut in how you respond to them.

After you've chosen the music, find a comfortable place to sit. While each piece of music is playing, really concentrate on how it feels in your body. What kind of responses does it stimulate in you? Do you want to relax or dance, cry or laugh, sing along or jump up and turn it off?

Whatever the response is, notice it. Then ask yourself; "Is this response something that would be in the highest good for myself and all concerned?" If so, do it! Get up and dance, laugh out loud or cry.

By mindfully doing something we often take for granted, we can familiarize ourselves with how it feels to be emotionally triggered by a stimulus. This can help us learn to understand how it feels to choose to relax and simply observe our response to the stimulus or to choose to get up and dance to the energy awakened within us.

Asking this question of yourself about "the highest good for all" during this activity can create another anchor you can use to remember to be mindful in highly stimulating situations. As soon as you notice that your emotions are being stimulated, you can remember to ask yourself this question and become mindful of the response that arises within you. Mindfulness activities such as this can significantly improve our ability to choose what we want to do when we feel anger rising within us.

# MINDFULNESS AND MONEY

Money is a funny thing for most of us. We all know we want it and yet we can never seem to get enough of it. One reason for this is that money is based on a scarcity model in most cultures on the planet. You've most likely heard sayings like there's not enough to go around, it's a dog eat dog world, it's survival of the fittest, etc. The list goes on and on. With this mindset it seems that getting more money is the only solution for many of the things that cause us stress. This keeps us striving for more and more of it. But what for; to get more toys, a bigger house or more money in the bank? So we can achieve some level of social recognition or power? So we can have more safety and security for ourselves and our family?

Now don't get me wrong, I believe that money is a wonderful thing. Without it we would still be trading chickens and goats in order to meet our needs. And the exchange of energy represented by money – when in the hands of those who use it mindfully – has the power to once and for all change the world for the better.

But just chasing the elusive dream of financial freedom by itself, without being mindful in relation to money, keeps us striving for more and more money and yet never be satisfied that we have enough because we don't know what freedom truly means. More often than not, our worries about money come from the belief that without it we are in some way inadequate – that how much money we have is a measure of our worth. This mindless relationship with money is why many of us feel stressed out, overworked, and dissatisfied. But there is a better way! We can begin to approach financial matters more mindfully.

Regardless of our financial situation, we must first be present and grateful for what we have before the door will open for more. This is reflected in the old saying that what we resist persists, which is just another way of saying that what we focus our attention on will grow. If we're always focused on what's wrong with our present conditions – on lack, limitation, and fear – then we're resisting the present moment, and bound to get a lot more of what we're resisting.

## THREE MINDFULNESS EXERCISES TO HELP WITH YOUR FINANCES

### One - Allow What Is

Every time you feel inadequate, or are envious of something you do not have, stop for a moment, and breathe deeply. Recognize and feel these emotions within you. Take a moment to consider your situation without resistance. What would your life be like without the beliefs that cause you this kind of stress? Are you really inadequate if you don't get a new car (house, job, boyfriend/girlfriend, pair of shoes…) this year? Do you really need this right now, in this moment? Are you suffering from the lack of it? The answer to this question – and many more like it – is most probably a resounding 'no'. Next become very conscious of your immediate surroundings. Can you find anything in your environment that is beautiful, interesting or intriguing?

Notice everything. Is the rug on the floor soft under your feet? Does the air moving in and out your nostrils feel cool and fresh? There is always something to enjoy – something to be grateful for – if you look for it. Now move out into your life a little further and consider all of your present life conditions. What else is there in your circumstances, your relationships, and the other aspects of your life that you can acknowledge and be grateful for in the present moment?

When we are able to allow 'what is' to just 'be,' without a lot of emotional upheaval, and to be present to and grateful for all the wonderful things that we do have in our lives, then, and only then is there room for more abundance to come to us.

## Two - Take Stock

One other reason why finances are often such a source of pain and panic is due to the fact that we avoid thinking about them. We actively put money out of our mind as much as possible as we become scared of addressing problems in our situation, and what the condition of our finances actually represents.

Have you ever avoided looking at your bank balance? Most of us have. But any problem reflected in your bank balance is something that would be best tended to sooner rather than later.

One way to overcome this pattern of behavior is by purposefully putting aside a few minutes each day to mindfully address the existence of your financial life and your feelings about money. As an opportunity to practice the ABCs of mindfulness, make a commitment to keeping your checkbook balanced. Perform the entire process while staying aware of each of the ABCs. If specific issues or concerns arise during this practice then make a list of these and then set aside a time to mindfully consider each one. This is a simple way to create a mindful relationship with your finances.

By mindfully acknowledging our financial situation, we can gain more clarity on the subject, create more financial responsibility, discover and take actions that are needed for our financial health, and begin to reduce the time we spend worrying about money.

## Three - Give, Give, and Give Some More

Money is just energy, but unfortunately the majority of money on this planet is either being hoarded away or moved around by people with a scarcity / survival of the fittest / us-against-them mindset. I believe that the world won't change until people just like us – those devoted to creating more mindfulness in the world – start moving money around with love and caring energy behind their choices. Maintaining this energy is an excellent way of being mindful about money.

There is a wonderful practice that I learned from author Edwene Gaines. My modified version is called Spontaneous Giving. This practice entails giving – in the form of money – to anyone who helps you feel inspired, brings joy to your life or enlightens you in some way. This is different than giving to charity, which is giving because there is a need. Giving charitably is perfectly fine – but it's different than Spontaneous Giving, which is about giving to individual people or organizations that bring more abundance to your life.

What I mean by abundance is an abundance of joy, hope, courage, inspiration, love, caring, etc. Spontaneous Giving is the movement of energy, in the form of money, with the movement itself being propelled by the energy of abundance. I strongly believe that as more and more money starts moving around with the energy of love and inspiration behind it, that this will quite literally and dramatically change the world – and contribute to your personal abundance as well.

To begin this money mindfulness practice all you need is to determine what percentage of your income you are comfortable practicing with, and then start carrying this money around to give away. This can be whatever you are comfortable with, 1%, 5%, 10%, or more, and it can be in the form of a check or it can be $5, $10, and $20 bills. Again, whatever you feel comfortable with.

After you have your intention in mind and cash in hand, during your daily activities become very mindful about when you are touched, moved or inspired. Look for those moments when someone's actions or an organization's activities – either a for-profit or nonprofit – contribute to your sense of living in an abundant world. Look for those times when you say to yourself, "I wish more of that happened in the world." When you notice, stop and tell them exactly what they did that touched, moved or inspired you and then contribute to them in whatever amount that you are moved to, an amount that adequately expresses how deeply you were touched moved or inspired. If it's an organization of some sort, write them a letter that explains clearly what they've done that has motivated you to send them this contribution.

Time after time this exercise has brought me more love, more joy, and more fulfillment than I have ever known. The connection between me and the other person in that present moment has always been deep and incredibly touching.

Can you imagine what an abundant and prosperous world this would be if everybody turned their attention away from what was wrong in the world or not working in their lives, and instead started to become mindful of what touched, moved, and inspired them? Then, with that same level of mindfulness, acknowledged that person for their inspiration with a gift of money given with the energy of love. Imagine a world where the energy that moved the money was that of love, inspiration, and acknowledgment, rather than lack, limitation, and fear.

I highly recommend this practice.

# CONCLUSION

More and more professional psychologists, mental health specialists, and those who are experts in related fields are recommending mindfulness as a regular practice to people of all walks of life. This is because the benefits of this ancient and profound way of being and way of living are becoming increasingly clear. The mind will never cease to amaze us, and there has never been a more important time to allow it to shine, to awaken to the present moment, and bask in the beauty of the here and now.

Mindfulness is a powerful tool when it comes to managing our lives, solving our problems, and dealing with worries about the future or regrets of the past. By being more mindful we wake up to the reality of the world. When we leave the past as it is, and understand that the future is more or less unknowable, we can let things be as they are and allow ourselves to exist within the beauty of the moment.

We need to come to terms with the fact, no matter how difficult such a leap of faith may appear, that we do ourselves no favor by reliving the past, by dwelling in the unknown or creating fearful scenarios of the future. Only when we relax, get present, and become mindful do we live a happier, healthier, and more successful life.

I have covered a few of my favorite mindfulness exercises and meditations in this book, but there are dozens more to explore, and many different mindfulness methods to utilize. However, when it comes to mindfulness, we all have one thing in common. In order to experience the most wonderful life possible, we need to live the life we have in the present moment, and to do this we need to gain insights into what life means and what living really is. Life is wonderful, and it would be such a shame to miss it because we're not paying attention.

# AFTERWORD

Remember to get your free *101 Ways to Meditate*. Used in conjunction with *The Meditation for Life Series*, this supplementary resource will help you find the perfect ways for you to achieve a successful meditative state, tranquility, relaxation, peace of mind, and much more.

www.BethBanningAuthor.com/101-Meditations-Sign-Up

**PS** – Thank you again for purchasing this book. I hope you found it valuable. If so, please *Write a Review* on Amazon. I greatly appreciate your feedback and your review will help others know if this book is right for them.

# ABOUT THE AUTHOR

By the young age of 16 Beth had experienced so many people barely surviving that it became her passion and mission to help people thrive.

She took this passion into her work and co-founded Focused Attention, Inc. She is also the author of numerous books including; *The Marriage Guide Series*, the *Meditation for Life Series* and the forthcoming book *Interviewed by God* - **A Spiritual Odyssey of Awakening**. She has also Co-created the *Pathway to Personal Freedom* and the *Art of Conscious Connection Seminar Series* with her spiritual and life partner Neill Gibson.

Collectively, Beth and Neill share over 60 years of experience exploring and synthesizing the work of many spiritual leaders and experts in the human potential movement. They draw on this experience to offer concrete, practical skills that help people exchange ideas and resources in harmony with their most deeply held values.

Beth has inspired thousands of people around the world to change their personal and professional paradigms from the current norm of "the survival of the fittest" to a Power of We mindset, which is fundamental to the new consciousness emerging on the planet.

Made in the USA
Lexington, KY
12 May 2014